An Arab Family

LIBRARY OF CONGRESS CATALOGING IN PUBLICATION DATA

Dutton, Roderic.
 An Arab family.

 Rev. ed. of: Arab village. 1980.
 Summary: Depicts life in a small village in Oman.
 1. Al Khābūrah (Oman)—Juvenile literature.
2. Oman—Social life and customs—Juvenile literature.
[1. Oman—Social life and customs] I. Free, John
Brand, ill. II. Title.
DS248.A44D87   1985   953'.53   85-10272
ISBN 0-8225-1660-8 (lib. bdg.)

Manufactured in the United States of America

 2   3   4   5   6   7   8   9   10   95   94   93   92   91   90   89   88   87   86

An Arab Family

Roderic Dutton

Photographs by John B. Free

Lerner Publications Company · Minneapolis

This is Mohammed. He lives with his family in the village of Khabura on the shores of the Indian Ocean. Khabura is in Oman, a country on the tip of the Arabian Peninsula.

Mohammed and his wife Zainab have six sons and three daughters. The youngest boy is still a baby, and the two oldest girls are already married. Hadiga, the only unmarried daughter, lives at home and helps take care of the house.

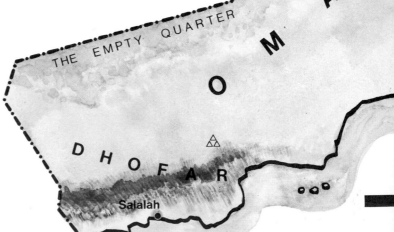

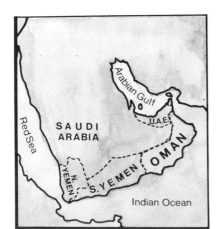

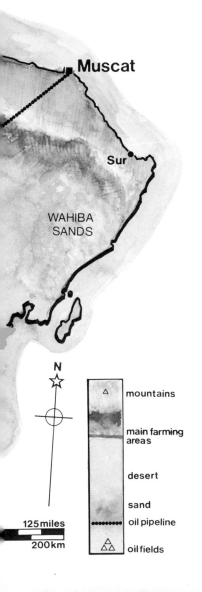

Muscat

Sur

WAHIBA
SANDS

N
☆

125 miles
200 km

△	mountains
	main farming areas
	desert
	sand
••••••	oil pipeline
△△	oil fields

Zainab does all the cooking over an open fire. She uses lots of pots and pans, which Hadiga later scrubs clean. They have no electric stoves or washing machines to make housework easier.

When Mohammed is out, Zainab sometimes invites her women friends over for coffee. They eat dates and discuss the local news.

Zainab owns a sewing machine, and she and Hadiga use it to make their clothes. The women in Oman wear beautiful, brightly colored dresses over loose-fitting trousers. The men wear long white robes, which they buy from the tailors in the village market.

When Mohammed's first child was born, there weren't any schools in Khabura. But in 1970, Sultan Qaboos became Ruler of Oman, and he had many schools built. Now all the children in the village go to school. Mahmoud, Mohammed's oldest son, works hard and hopes to become a doctor or an airline pilot one day.

There are many new buildings in Khabura, all built using concrete blocks. Houses used to be made of date palm leaves, knotted together by hand. Now workshops in every village make concrete blocks.

Khabura also has a new electric power plant. Mohammed hopes to have electricity in his home soon. Then he can install electric lights in his house and maybe even buy some modern appliances.

Mohammed's house stands in the middle of a tiny farm. Here Mohammed grows dates, limes, mangoes, and bananas.

The dates ripen during the hot summer months and are picked by men who climb the date palm trees. Some of the dates are eaten fresh. The rest are dried in the sun and saved for winter.

Most of the limes are dried and sold to a man in the village market. Mohammed keeps some fresh limes because his family likes to squeeze the juice over rice and meat.

There are also two goats in Mohammed's yard. Many people in the village keep a few animals. They might have a cow that they milk or a goat that they plan to eat at a festival.

9

Very little rain falls on the gardens of Khabura. Usually, it rains only three or four days out of the whole year. Some years there is no rain at all.

But rain does fall on the mountains, which are inland. That water seeps into the earth and flows underground toward the coast. The villagers dig wells to get enough water to drink, wash, and water their crops.

Water for the crops is pumped out of the wells by engines. In Mohammed's yard, water flows into a concrete basin. The children often use it as a pool to play in.

Then the water flows through a network of small ditches to water the crops. Without these ditches, the gardens would be as dry as the plains around Khabura.

One crop which needs a regular supply of water is alfalfa. It is grown as food for the animals. Farmers can also earn money by selling alfalfa for high prices to neighboring Arab countries.

Everyone who lives in Khabura is Muslim. The high point of their year is Ramadan, the holy month of fasting. During this month Muslims don't eat or drink anything during the hours of daylight.

At the end of Ramadan, there is a big celebration. The people of Khabura dance in the square by the old fort.

Mohammed makes a special meal for his family and friends. Just before the end of Ramadan he buys a goat at the market. He kills the goat and then prepares it for cooking while his friend carefully rubs salt into the goatskin to preserve it. Later on, the skin will be made into a leather bag. It will be used as a churn, to separate butter from cows' milk.

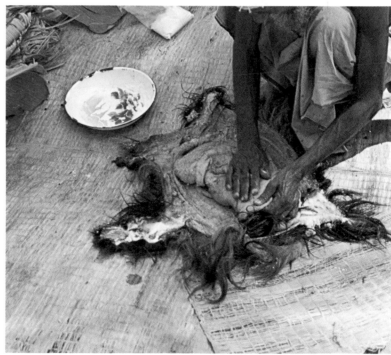

Most of the meat is cooked in a *tanour*. A *tanour* is a hole in the ground that is used as an oven. Mohammed lights a fire in the *tanour* and lets it become very hot. He wraps the meat in leaves, waits until the fire turns to ashes, and then throws the packages of meat into the *tanour*.

The hole is then covered with earth to keep the heat in and left for 24 hours. When Mohammed takes the meat out of the *tanour*, it is ready to eat.

Families in Khabura usually eat together. But on a special occasion like this one, the women eat separately from the men.

The men sit on the ground, around a big central dish heaped with meat, rice, and dates. Afterwards, they eat fruit and *halwa* and drink strong black coffee.

Halwa, also called halvah, is a flaky, sweet dessert usually made of crushed sesame seeds and honey.

Mohammed's oldest daughter, Fatima, and her husband, Rashid, live in the nearby village of Khuwayrat. In Khuwayrat, most men are part-time fishermen. If they catch a lot of fish, they take them to the market in Khabura to be sold.

Rashid comes from a fishing family. He and his brother own two small boats. They are made from date palm leaves and have been built in the same way for hundreds of years.

Rashid doesn't always have time to fish, because he also owns a store and a workshop that makes concrete blocks. But when the brothers think there are plenty of fish, they take their boats to sea. Then they spread the nets and set their traps.

Sometimes shoals of sardines swim near the shore. Fishermen in boats lower nets around the fish. Then everyone in the village wades into the sea to pull the nets ashore. The sardines are spread out on the beach to dry in the sun.

    Many of the palm leaf fishing boats used to have sails. Others were rowed with oars. Now many of the boats have engines and rarely will a fisherman row.

    Some fishermen use larger wooden boats. These boats can carry more nets and bring back more fish. They can stay longer out at sea, but are heavy to pull up on to the beach. All the wooden boats have big engines.

    Recently, fisherman have been buying light metal boats from the government. They like these boats because they are cheap and easy to carry ashore.

The fishermen in Khuwayrat catch most of their fish at night or very early in the morning. In the afternoon, they repair their nets, sometimes with the help of the whole family. The beach is covered with floats, nets, anchors, and wire fish traps.

These traps are made in the village. One day two of Mohammed's cousins came to Khabura and asked if he would find some fishing traps for them. They knew that the craftsmen in the fishing villages near Khabura make good traps at reasonable prices.

One of the trap-makers agreed to make the traps but explained that the price would be higher than Mohammed had paid because the cost of the wire had risen sharply. Mohammed still thought the trap-maker was asking too much. The two men discussed the situation until they finally agreed on a price.

Mohammed does most of the family food shopping. Each week he goes to the market in the center of Khabura to buy rice, flour, coffee, fruit, and *halwa*.

He buys fish from the market every day. He either buys a piece of fish from a fish trader or a whole fish from one of the boats as it arrives in the market.

The market has grown very rapidly in recent years. New shops have been built and there is now a wide choice of goods. Villagers can buy radios, canned food, and even children's bicycles.

Mohammed used to own more land than he does now, and he employed people to work on it. Now the young men who worked for him have joined the army, where they can earn more money.

Mohammed is still an important man in the village. His opinions are trusted, and he is often asked to settle arguments between neighbors.

Recently, Mohammed bought a small truck. He drives this to big towns like Muscat or Dubai, which is in the neighboring country of the United Arab Emirates. He buys building materials or fruit and rice and brings them back to Khabura. Then he resells them in the market at a higher price.

A few years ago, Mohammed would have bought a camel, not a truck. "Camel trains" were once a common sight, but now trucks transport most goods.

In the past, people often traveled around on donkeys. Today they use cars, and donkeys are usually only used to carry children to school.

Life began to change in Khabura when oil was discovered in Oman. Japan, the United States, and countries in Europe pay a very high price for the oil, so there is much more money in Oman than there used to be. Now oil tankers are a familiar sight from the shoreline.

The government uses some of the money to help villages like Khabura. The government has built the electric power plant, new roads, and new schools and has provided tractors for the farmers.

There are also new jobs in the large towns. Many young people from the villages go to work in these towns. They send money home to their families, who use it to buy concrete blocks, trucks, and engines for fishing boats.

When Mohammed's children leave school, they will probably go away to work and send back money to their parents. Mohammed and Zainab can look forward to a comfortable old age.

The Nations of the Arab World

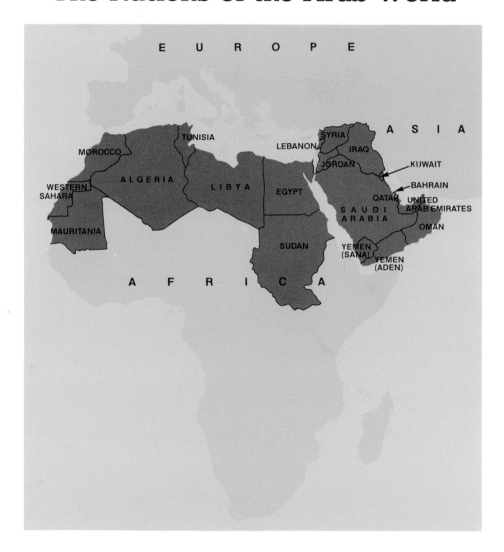

Facts about Arabs

Arabs live in many other countries besides Oman. All told, 19 nations make up the Arab world.

Seven of these countries are on the continent of Africa. They are Mauritania, Morocco, Algeria, Tunisia, Libya, Egypt, and the Sudan. Arabs also live in the area of Western Sahara.

The remaining 12 countries are on the Arabian Peninsula or are situated to its north. They are Saudi Arabia, the United Arab Emirates, Qatar, Oman, Yemen (Aden), and Yemen (Sana), Lebanon, Syria, Jordan, Iraq, Kuwait, and Bahrain. Yemen (Aden) and Yemen (Sana) are also called South Yemen and North Yemen. Together with Egypt and the Sudan, the 12 Arab countries on or near the Arabian Peninsula are referred to as "the Middle East."

The 19 nations of the Arab world are home to about 150 million Arabs. They all share the same language, Arabic, and the same culture. But they differ from one another in many other ways. Most Arabs are Muslims, but some are Christians. Some Arabs have dark skin, and others have light skin.

Some Arabs are nomads and live as they have for centuries, while others live in cities and have adopted Western ways. Many, like Mohammed and his family, are somewhere in the middle, combining their traditional ways with modern ones.

NORTH
AMERICA

SOUTH
AMERICA

EUROPE

A S I A

AFRICA

Arab
Countries

AUSTRALIA

31

Families the World Over

Some children in foreign countries live like you do. Others live very differently. In these books, you can meet children from all over the world. You'll learn about their games and schools, their families and friends, and what it's like to grow up in a faraway land.

A FAMILY IN CHINA	A FAMILY IN PAKISTAN	A FAMILY IN BRAZIL
A FAMILY IN EGYPT	A FAMILY IN SRI LANKA	A FAMILY IN CHILE
A FAMILY IN FRANCE	A FAMILY IN WEST GERMANY	A FAMILY IN IRELAND
A FAMILY IN INDIA	AN ABORIGINAL FAMILY	A FAMILY IN MOROCCO
A FAMILY IN JAMAICA	AN ARAB FAMILY	A FAMILY IN SINGAPORE
A FAMILY IN NIGERIA	AN ESKIMO FAMILY	A ZULU FAMILY

Lerner Publications Company
241 First Avenue North
Minneapolis, Minnesota 55401